Grief

Journal

Written and Illustrated by

Linda Lodge Abelson Andreozzi

A *HeartWisdom*™ Self-Guided Retreat Journal

from Cabin 6, Inc.

Published by

Good Ground Press

To

John Andreozzi
with love and gratitude.

And To

Gregory Alan Abelson,
Jean Work Lodge,
James Robert Lodge,
and Re,
in loving memory.

Design and Graphic
Production by Cabin 6, Inc.
Cabin6inc@aol.com

Artwork photographed
by Don Loegering.

ISBN: 1-885996-10-1
Copyright © 2002
by Linda Andreozzi.

Good Ground Press
1884 Randolph Avenue,
St. Paul, MN 55105.

800-232-5533
goodgroundpress.com
griefjournal.com

Where to go

Journal through the forest of grief.

I worked late that night; it was 9:32 when I got home, walked in the front door, and went down the hall to the kitchen. I set my tote bag on the floor, turned, and my life changed forever. *Why was he on the floor, with his back up against the stove? "Greg?"* I knelt beside him, looked into his blank stare, and felt for his pulse... none. In silent slow-motion I called 911, laid him down on the floor and began CPR. As I pushed air in and out of his lungs, his lips fluttered as if he were breathing. Moving air is not breathing. I began to taste the salt of his blood in my mouth. *"No! Don't go!"* I screamed to the ceiling.

My husband, Greg, was dead at the age of thirty-three.

That night my life was picked up from one path and dropped onto another. I felt alone in a dark forest. I couldn't see a path, but I started to walk.

Two years later, in the back of a Chinatown grocery store, I found a journal with a crimson brocade cover. It chose me. I didn't even know I was looking for a journal, but I began to write. Now, fourteen years, fourteen journals later, I look back and I see a path.

Writing in my journal felt good. I could say things I didn't want to share with my sisters, friends, or therapist. My thoughts and feelings were private, embarrassing, and confusing – important only to me. My journal listened; it didn't judge or tell me what to do. At night I reread my journal like a bedtime storybook, then tucked it under my pillow, and shut my eyes. It became my companion.

Grief Journal is my offering to you – a companion. It's also a partnership. Journal through the forest of your grief and side-by-side our stories will unfold. In each section I tell my story; then you're invited to reflect on your own feelings and tell *your* story. Look, listen, and consider what you write in this journal: you may find a path toward peace and acceptance of the loss in your life. You have begun.

Make it safe.

Protect your journal.

When I was a little girl, my teenage sisters had diaries with locks and keys. I wouldn't have looked in their diaries even without the locks. Respect for privacy was learned early in our family. We four girls shared bedrooms in our small house and it was important for my sisters to know their secrets were safe. Now, as adults, my sisters and I have promised that our journals marked 'private' will not be read after we die. I may have them burn mine. That assurance opens my heart to write in my journals with rigorous honesty and candor.

A journal is a vessel for the intimacies of the soul. When I believe someone else is going to read my journal, I edit and censor my thoughts and feelings. Then, my writing is no longer fresh, honest, or useful.

If you live with others, this may be a concern. No simple lock on my sisters' diaries would have kept out a sibling, friend, or parent who wanted to get in, but the intruder would have known they were breaking a trust.

Create your journal's protective boundary. This boundary may be marked with a statement as simple as "This is my private journal." Consider where you store it; perhaps an underwear drawer or nightstand says "private" in your home. Write a message on the journal flyleaf that requests the book remain unread by others – now and in the future.

How comfortable am I writing in this journal with honesty and candor?

_____

_____

Who else is likely to look at it? Why?

_____

_____

_____

_____

_____

Where will I keep this journal?

How clear are others that my journal is out of bounds and private?

I remember a time when my privacy wasn't respected. It was when...

I felt...

Bring a light.

Protect yourself.

As I entered my living room, I felt as if I were dying. It was a late night in a cold February. I had just returned from the hospice where my mother lay in her last days of ovarian cancer. She, my closest friend, was dying a painful death. I was a recent widow. Her symptoms had begun on the day of my husband's funeral. Pain – how inadequate that word is.

Earlier that evening, I talked about my pain with a group of people I didn't know well. They seemed to pull back from me. *Was I too intense for them?* Rejected, lonely, sad, scared, lost – I felt as if I were in a big black hole and couldn't feel the floor beneath my feet. I was 35 and I had never made a spiritual nest. It was the darkest moment of my life.

Other than prewritten church prayers, and little bribes to a God I wasn't sure about, I had never truly prayed. From the bottom of my black hole, I looked up and prayed, straight from my heart, one whispered word: *help.* Before the word was fully-formed, the phone rang. I laughed and thought, *That's funny, I prayed and a bell rang.* It was 10:30 pm, no one called me that late. I answered and heard the voice of a friend I worked with years before. He said he called to see how I was. He had been through a similar time in his life; he listened and understood. He was comforting. God called me on the telephone. That call began my prayer life. I still use that good one word prayer: *help.*

A prayer from your heart can be your light in darkness. You can't lose it. It's always there for you when you need it, *no matter what.*

Oh , God,

my God,

wrap me

in your loving arms;

clasp me

to your breast,

rock me gently

in the dark;

hold me

'til I rest.

Amen

5

Light the Light.

Write a prayer for yourself.

Look into your heart and choose your own words of protection, acceptance, healing, and love. Ask for exactly what you need. For example, if I'm worried about opening a painful memory as I write or if I'm exposing my feelings in a group, I might pray:

> *Oh, God, please help me. These wounds still hurt, and I'm afraid to open them up again. Hold me close. I need your comfort and love. Amen*

There are also silent, wordless prayers as in centering or contemplative prayer. Sometimes, movement becomes my prayer. It's the doing or being of the prayer that's important; prayer doesn't need words. Whichever form you prefer, use prayer in this journal experience when you feel vulnerable. You may want to try it as you begin or end each session.

Some suggestions:

- *Keep it simple*
- *Use your own words*
- *Remember it's just for you*
- *Ask for what you need*
- *Try silence*
- *Remember a childhood prayer*

- *Consider whom you're addressing – God, Holy Spirit, Great Spirit, Higher Power, Jesus, Goddess, Buddha, unnamed source of wisdom and life*
- *Pray as if you know how if praying is new to you or as if you believe if you doubt*

I remember when I was very young I prayed…

_____

_____

_____

_____

_____

My own prayer of protection and comfort is…

_____

_____

_____

_____

_____

_____

_____

_____

Search for the words.

Journaling tools

It's the tools you *aren't* going to use that are most important – penmanship, spelling, punctuation, accuracy, neatness, sentence form, or any other writing skill that makes you pause to examine your words. Allow yourself to let go of your inner editor and judge. You've already made your journal safe; no one else is going to read it. Start writing and don't reread until later.

Honesty, courage, and humor are powerful journaling tools. I seek privacy, quiet, and comfort as I write. A regular allotted time helps make journaling a habit, even a ritual. While grieving my husband's death, the ten minutes I spent with my journal each night was often the best part of my day.

"Hot penning" is one way to get started. If you are feeling stuck or overwhelmed, this method may help release thoughts and feelings from the heart. Move from your head into your heart. Don't plan what you are going to write, these words are feelings.

To begin hot penning, put your pen to paper and start moving it. You may want to use the blank sheets in the back of this journal or doodle on separate pages to get started. You could draw loops (like the Palmer Method practice) or write "blah blah blah blah" – whatever flows out of your pen. For 20 minutes, continue to move your pen, don't stop, don't take your pen off the paper. The words will will begin to flow: a heartstream.

Tell your story.

Mother sat on a stool beside her phone and leaned against the wall. Her husband, my father, had died in the night, just hours before. She dialed the next friend on her list, and I knew her next words. She told the story again. She repeated the same details on each call: the wonderful steak dinner, the glass of wine they shared before bed, odd breathing that woke her, the paramedics and the stretcher that didn't fit through the door. I came into the story at the hospital waiting room where we heard together the doctor's awful words... *"Mrs. Lodge, I'm sorry to tell you..."* I wondered how many more times she'd need to tell *The Story*. I was young and I didn't understand. Yet.

Nine years later it was my turn. *"I worked late that night; it was 9:32 when I got home, walked in the front door, and went down the hall to the kitchen. I set my tote bag on the floor, turned, and my life changed forever."* That began *my* story. I've told it over and over again. In the beginning, I told clerks in stores, people on elevators, and anyone else who was in my presence for more than a minute. It helped me to tell my story. All the details were important to me: our last words were *"I love you,"* our last meal was a halved pear. I held on to every detail, and I still have them tucked inside my heart.

A year after my husband died, I was sitting around a campfire with our old friends. Talking through my tears, I was well into the telling of my "It was 9:32 when I came home" story, when midsentence, I looked at my friend, saw a knowing look, and it hit me: *"Oh, you know this story, don't you."* She smiled. And now, years later, when a good friend or sister gives me the gift of listening, I tell my story. Again.

Now, please, tell your story — with all the details.

This is what happened.

Embrace friends, suffer fools.

Friends will find you.

I was lost in a kitchen full of people who loved me. It was the same kitchen in which my husband died a few days before. Time had stopped, yet others went on with their lives as if life hadn't ended. The refrigerator beside me was stuffed with food, but I hadn't eaten since he died. I didn't know how to open the fridge door, choose something to eat, or put it on a plate.

My friend, Patty, came to the front door, plate in hand. On the plate was a ham sandwich. She put the plate in my hand and said, *"Here... eat this."* Patty's ham sandwich was a sacrament of friendship – communion. I hadn't told anyone that I couldn't put food on a plate and move it to my mouth. I don't know if Patty knew that; she knew what to do and did it.

Often it's easier to give than to receive. But I learned to let go, and I was given much. My sisters cried with me, laughed with me, and became my lifelong friends. My friend Peter appeared at my door when he was worried about the sound of my voice on the phone. Unexpected people came forward with grace and help. I saw my friends and family like a stand of trees, shoulder to shoulder. Some of them stepped forward, some didn't move, and a few others stepped back or out. The people who stepped forward knew grief. I don't begrudge those who didn't step forward; I'm grateful for the ones who could and did.

People say foolish things.

A month after my husband died, a woman told me that I should be done with crying, that my grief had gone on too long. *Was I being self-indulgent? Was I doing it wrong?* I didn't know. Now, I can laugh at her foolish comment. Then, I felt angry, hurt and scared. Others said: *"He's better off." "I know exactly how you feel." "Don't feel sad." "Don't cry."* I wanted to say *"You don't know he's better off." "You don't know how I feel." "I am sad."* and *"I am going to cry."* But, I didn't know how to say what I felt. Talk that normally only bothered me, became intolerable. It was difficult for me to listen to trivialities, gossip, or office politics. Of course, *I* was difficult.

Grief is difficult.

Who are my friends? Do they know grief? Who has stepped forward?

_____

_____

_____

_____

_____

_____

It really helped me when...

_____

_____

_____

_____

_____

It's hard for me to listen to, hear about, or discuss...

_____

_____

_____

_____

_____

_____

_____

What could I ask for that people don't know I need?

_____

_____

_____

_____

Raw pain

I was shocked by the blue body. My father was empty without his spirit. He was laid out on a table in the county hospital. I stood alone beside him and whispered, *"I'm here, Dad, I love you."* His death was my first great loss, and my first dead body. I began to shake. I continued to shake at the graveside. But, I've never been able to shake that final image of my father's blue body.

That's why, years later, in another county hospital, I didn't go in to see my husband after the doctors had ripped his chest open. They couldn't bring him back to life, and I didn't need to say goodbye to another blue body. Instead, I walked down the corridor to the bathroom. At the steel sink I ran cold water on my hands, splashed my face, and looked at the stranger in the mirror, me. I was separate from myself, disassociated. Like the shock of a fall into cold deep water, I felt the ring of silence press against my ears as I sank. *How do I survive?* Breathe – that much I knew. And then, something unexpected, unfamiliar, began to flow into me, strength and comfort. I felt the presence of God.

In the next months I, a skinless mass of exposed nerve-endings, was furious that my husband, also my best friend and comforter, wasn't there to help me or to hold me at night in the dark. I needed *him* to help me through the grief of his loss. Grief isn't logical.

Grief takes time, and we each take our own amount of time. There is no right amount. The raw pain will last somewhere from a month to a year. Ignore or bury the pain, and it will last longer. During the first year's dreaded "firsts" in the cycle of birthdays, anniversaries, and holidays, I told myself before each:*"That's the last time I have to do that for the first time."* It seemed to help me – I believe simple things often work well.

Notice what helps you. Learn to be good to yourself and keep your life as simple as possible. Be with friends, but also make sure to spend time alone. No matter what you do, time passes. Each breath marks a passage of healing time and puts a distance between the present moment and the moment of your loss. Since you're reading this, you've probably moved beyond your "skinless, raw-nerve-endings" stage. If so, note the distance you've come along your path – you're surviving.

Then Jonah prayed to the Lord his God
from the belly of the fish, saying,

"I called to the Lord out of my distress,
and God answered me; out of the belly of
Sheol I cried, and you heard my voice.

You cast me into the deep,
into the heart of the seas,
and the flood surrounded me;
all your waves and your
billows passed over me.

Then I said,
'I am driven away from your sight;
how shall I look again upon
your holy temple?'

The waters closed in over me;
the deep surrounded me;
weeds were wrapped around
my head at the roots of the
mountains.

I went down to the land
whose bars closed upon me forever;
yet you brought up my life
from the pit,
O Lord my God.

As my life was ebbing away, I
remembered the Lord; and my prayer
came to you, into your holy temple."

Jonah 2:1-7 (NRSV)

15

At first I felt...

_____

_____

_____

_____

_____

_____

_____

_____

_____

_____

_____

_____

_____

_____

How long has it been? What feels different to me now?

_____

_____

_____

_____

When pain feels raw, it really helps me to...

_____

_____

_____

_____

_____

I remember other pain from the past, such as...

_____

_____

_____

_____

_____

_____

_____

_____

_____

_____

_____

_____

_____

_____

_____

_____

_____

_____

_____

_____

_____

_____

_____

_____

_____

Celebrate the life.

Greg.

When I knew him as a boy,
I saw the man in him.
Then, he became the man,
and I loved the boy in him.

He cried when he heard Dr. King speak or saw a dead rabbit in the road.
But, he always tried to make me laugh and I always laughed.

I loved his blonde hair, the twinkle in his eye, and his knobby, skinny legs.

He made a hole in my coat pocket and held my hand on the way to school each day.

He took apart everything to see how it worked
and sometimes got it back together again.

He said "I love you" right out loud from the phone at work.

He gave me the crusts off his pizza.
He slept beside me like a spoon and hugged me in his sleep.

He squeezed my nose, he tickled me, he squirted me with water.
He held me when my father died.

He played guitar too loud and danced to a rhythm I never could find.

He was tender, he was kind, he was outrageous.
He was strong, he was brave, he was a genius.

He loved me. And I love him forever.

I wrote this the day after he died and read it at his funeral. It flowed
out of my pen in a heartstream. Love floats like a leaf boat on that
heartstream, its cargo the wisp of magic that is in the spirit of love.

Write a eulogy to your lost love.

Celebrate that life – remember all the quirks and the little things you
loved. Capture the spirit and let it flow from your heart through your pen.
Whether a leaf or a whole barge, float a boat of love on your heartstream.

These are the things I loved and now I miss:

_____
_____
_____
_____
_____
_____
_____
_____
_____
_____
_____
_____
_____
_____
_____
_____
_____
_____

These things bothered me and I don't miss them:

_____
_____
_____
_____
_____
_____
_____

The silence of yarn

Blue

She wound another skein of blue yarn into a ball and tossed it onto the mound beside me. Mom couldn't talk much – ovarian cancer had sent tumors into her brain and affected her ability to string words into sentences. We talked without words or sentences in the silence of yarn. My hook moved through loops of soft wool, angora, and mohair forming my widow's cocoon. I wanted padding around me, and my hands wanted something to make. They made an afghan in colors of healing water: turquoise of the Caribbean, steel blue of Lake Superior, and a Pacific cobalt mixed with a little green seaweed. One foot of stitches for Mom's brain surgery, six inches for her chemotherapy, two feet of lonely nights in my empty house, four feet of crying, one foot of numbness, one foot of laughing with friends, and six inches of feeling sorry for myself. No one *needs* a 10-foot afghan. It became an outward and visible form of that painful first year. It's still beautiful.

Strawberry ice cream eaten right out of the box was another comfort. The difference between helping myself to feel better in good ways, and overindulging in self-destructive ways wasn't easy for me to judge. I believed I'd lost my reason for living when my husband died. When Mother began to die on the heels of his death, it was impossible for me to make judgments or be moderate. Death obscured the path of my life. Just about everyone I loved was gone. I thought I would die next, and soon.

True comfort

I found comfort in crocheting, strawberry ice cream... and scotch. All three made me feel better, but, neither yarn, ice cream, scotch, or this *Grief Journal*, can take the place of professional help. If you are wondering, as I was – *Can I bear this pain? How can I go on?* – it's time to contact a therapist or spiritual director. If you're using alcohol or drugs to ease your pain, this is the time to find lifelong sobriety through AA or other chemical dependency programs. It works. That's where I found my true comfort. But that's another story.

Consider dusting off an old skill, or try a new one that relaxes you, such as knitting, quilting, or woodworking. Occupy your hands in a way that lets your mind rest. Simple, mindless, repetitive movement was what I needed, not complex projects. Although for me colors and textures soothed, perhaps you're better suited to word puzzles or sorting desk drawers. Tying flies is relaxing for some. Simple woodworking, such as sanding, is simple and repetitive. It's not a task or job and doesn't need a result.

Nature has her own healing power: dig in the soil or weed a garden, gather and sort sticks for firewood. Collect stones or leaves for a bowl. Paint a wall. Fold paper birds.

Here are some things that might feel comforting for me:

_____

_____

_____

_____

_____

What overwhelms me? How overwhelmed do I feel?

_____

_____

_____

_____

How often do I go to food or alcohol for comfort?

_____

_____

How do I feel about seeking professional help?

_____

_____

_____

_____

Laugh in the dark.

I crawled into the bed in my mother's guest room. I was exhausted and dreaded her next morning's round of chemotherapy. There had been no break between my husband's abrupt death and the beginning of my Mother's two-year journey to death. I turned off the light and turned on, *Only When I Laugh*, my favorite BBC "Britcom." The comedy was set in the terminal ward of a hospital. It was *dark* humor, the only subject was death and dying – just my cup of tea. Mom was asleep in the next room. I laughed alone in the dark.

My idea of funny often alienated me from the rest of the world. People looked nervous when I laughed. Most people didn't want to look at death, talk about death, let alone *laugh* at it.

My sisters laughed with me, though. We laughed in hospital rooms with Mom hooked up to tubes and needles. She laughed with us, if only with her eyes, as we told the old family stories, the ones that live forever and aren't humorous to anyone who wasn't there. Life was rich with love in that laughter.

Often our attempts to care for Mom were futile and funny. My sisters and I laughed at our struggle to help her eat. We tried to make her food pretty or cajole her with tiny spoonfuls. We failed; all food tasted like metallic cardboard to her. The smell of what we liked to eat bothered her, and she didn't want it in the house. My sister Judy and I giggled like rebellious children as we broke her rules. Late one night we tossed a rope over the balcony rail and smuggled our favorite smelly pizza into her house.

Clean-up in Mom's kitchen always had precise rules. She instructed us, unseen, from her bed on the sofa: *"Now girls, be sure to put that tuna in the blue dish with the white cover." "Yes, Mom. OK, we'll do that,"* we said as we dumped her uneaten tuna down the disposal. That mutiny was a bittersweet turning-point for us. Judy and I laughed silent tears together over the sink.

Our laughter said, *"This is hard, but we're in it together."* In grief, laughter is a password only club members understand. It helps to have a club, even if you didn't choose to be a member.

Some things about this are really funny. Who can I laugh with?

_____

_____

_____

_____

_____

We would have laughed together at this...

_____

_____

_____

_____

_____

_____

I remember an old family story that always makes me laugh. It was when...

_____

_____

_____

_____

_____

_____

_____

_____

_____

_____

Parcel the grief.

See the rocks under the cedars in the painting? Mixed in with those rocks are the bones of my cat, Re. We'd been there together the previous year. We walked in the woods, worked a puzzle, read and took long afternoon naps together. He even painted with me, on that painting. He first came to live with me after my husband died. In that first year, when he would find me crying myself to sleep, he would curl up beside me and put his paw on my forehead.

Now, alone in the cabin behind those trees in the painting, I prepared to do my grief work. I hoped to end the week with a ritual, spreading Re's ashes among the rocks.

If you've never deeply loved an animal, it may be difficult for you to relate to the loss of a cat. One of the things I've learned along the path of grief is that sorrow is all the same. I loved that cat with all my heart.

In her book *Good Grief Rituals*, Elaine Childs-Gowell describes a process of putting a "bracket" on grief. I prefer to put it in a parcel. During my week alone, I parceled my grief for Re into a manageable size and opened it daily at a designated time. Then it no longer needed to be present in the back of all my thoughts asking for attention. When the thoughts appeared at other times of the day during the week, I said to them *"No, wait. At two o'clock I'll think about you."* At two o'clock, I would cry and remember the good times. Pain is easier to take in small doses, and I'm less apt to avoid it. So, for at least 15 minutes, each day, I thought of Re right down to his little pink toes and his shiny black fur – all the details that made my heart ache the most.

I still miss Re, but the parceling I did that week helped free some painful space around my heart.

24

I write this journal with the intention that it be useful for diverse forms of loss – death of a loved one, divorce, separation, change in life or health. Your grief may be very different from a loss through sudden death. My mother's death was slow, my husband's instantaneous, my cat's death a difficult decision. In all of the grief groups in which I've been a part, most of the participants were separated or divorced. At first I had to make a leap of faith that their pain was similar to my pain, and I had to translate their focus to my own. With time I saw that pain is pain – we each grieved loss.

As I wrote the section, *Embrace friends, suffer fools*, I watched the World Trade Center burn and collapse. I couldn't imagine the magnitude of grief born that morning. Each death leaves an empty space in the world that cannot be filled. I'm sad for all who lost a love on that day.

What are the losses in your life? List them below, and as you make your list, notice which ones still tighten your throat or bring a sting of tears to your eyes. Is it too painful to open the wound? Does that loss need a eulogy? (see *Celebrate the life*) Or does that loss need to be pulled out and put into a manageable parcel so you can accept it without being overwhelmed? Will you make a commitment to spend at least 15 minutes a day, for a week, to begin to free your heart of the painful thoughts that may linger in the background?

Grief wants to be heard and touched.

My Losses	*Still Painful*
	☐
	☐
	☐
	☐
	☐
	☐
	☐
	☐
	☐
	☐
	☐

Parceling: a week's worth

Choose a time each day this week: the same time each day if possible. Do this when and where you can be alone. You may want to use the time to think or cry, but writing will help you start. Let yourself remember. Be careful; use your prayer of protection. Light a candle. Take out a memento of the loss that has been too difficult to look at on your own. Spend at least 15 minutes, but no more than an hour. End with a peaceful salutation. Drink a glass of water. Shut your eyes in silence. Use what works best for you and begin.

What is my parcel of grief? _____

Monday __ / __ / __ Time: __:___

Light a candle. Say prayer of protection. Open the parcel.

_____

_____

_____

_____

_____

Tuesday __ / __ / __   Time: __:___

Light a candle. Say prayer of protection. Open the parcel.

_____

_____

_____

_____

_____

_____

_____

_____

Wednesday __ / __ / __   Time: __: ___

Light a candle. Say prayer of protection. Open the parcel.

_____

_____

_____

_____

_____

_____

Thursday __ / __ / __   Time: __: ___

Light a candle. Say prayer of protection. Open the parcel.

_____

_____

_____

_____

_____

_____

_____

Friday __ / __ / __   Time: __: ___

Light a candle. Say prayer of protection. Open the parcel.

_____

_____

_____

_____

_____

_____

Saturday __ / __ / __   Time: __: ___

Light a candle. Say prayer of protection. Open the parcel.

_____
_____
_____
_____
_____
_____
_____
_____
_____
_____
_____

Sunday __ / __ / __   Time: __: ___

Light a candle. Say prayer of protection. Open the parcel.

_____
_____
_____
_____
_____
_____
_____
_____
_____
_____
_____

What took me by surprise?

_____

_____

_____

_____

_____

_____

I think I still need to spend
some time with this part of
my grief:

_____

_____

_____

_____

_____

If I made a memorial to this
loss, it could be:

_____

_____

_____

_____

Reach out.

"Mother, I'd rather *do it myself!"* was a family joke, based on an old pain reliever ad on TV. We said it with a laugh, but we meant it in my family. My parents raised their daughters to be independent and then regretted it; we became very independent. From the beginning, I wanted to do everything myself, fix things alone and handle problems my way. Yes, I'm stubborn. I didn't like to ask for help. I thought that was my strength.

My *strength* weakened me; it almost did me in. After my husband died, followed by my mother, I was aware of the comfort and strength I received from God, but I still clung to my old brand of *"I'd rather do it myself"* strength. Before their deaths, I never read self-help books, joined support groups, or depended on a power greater than myself. As a widow, I liked it when people said, *"Oh, you're so strong, I don't know how you do it."* I buried the pain and got on with my life. I didn't have time to grieve. I had to work to keep my home. How could I stop for help?

Seven years after Greg's death I still struggled. The failure of new relationships showed me that buried pain doesn't go away. I used all my strength to push the grief under and move on, but it refused, popped out and told me I needed to do more work; work I couldn't do by myself. Finally, I reached out – *for* help and *to* help.

I reached out to help others in a grief support group ministry and began my real healing. It was a relief finally to be with people who understood from first-hand experience the pain of grief and loss. We formed easy, natural bonds. Our paths wouldn't have crossed otherwise; we were a wonderful ragtag, crazy quilt of wounded souls, driven by the same urge: to help others in pain. And that's how *we* were helped. I began to understand the paradoxical saying: *the only thing you know for sure that you can keep is what you give away.*

Helping heals – listening, talking, praying, crying, and hugging others in pain. I believe this is how God works in the world. To give and to receive is the same thing. God lives in the flow of love between helping and receiving hands. The work I've done talking and listening to others relieved my pain. Doing it myself, in my journal, was a start on the right path, but it wasn't enough. We need each other. Reach out.

When is the last time I helped someone in need? What do I have to give?

_____

_____

_____

_____

_____

_____

_____

_____

_____

_____

_____

Am I willing to admit I need help? What help do I need?

_____

_____

_____

_____

Where can I look for help?

_____

_____

_____

_____

_____

_____

_____

_____

Start again.

Each work day of my married life, I brought a bag from home and ate lunch in a small lunchroom with my work friends. They groaned and rolled their eyes with envy as I pulled out sandwiches on homemade baguettes with thin slices of roast, fresh fruit, a vegetable, and perhaps a piece of pie. My husband did all of the cooking, and he packed my lunches with love. Some people thought I was exaggerating when I said he did all the cooking; I wasn't. He loved to cook. It wasn't that I couldn't cook; I didn't.

After he died and the funeral food was gone, the refrigerator was full of empty wire shelves. On Mondays I ordered a pizza and the box sat alone on the wire shelves all week. Each night I stood in front of that door in the dark, stared inside the cold box, and thought: *Why? Why did he die?* (My hands go still in the memory of that bleak scene.)

He made all our holiday and party meals, so after his death I gave away the dining room table. I couldn't eat there. I could stand only a new simple wood table. With a placemat and flowers on the table, I lured myself to sit and eat alone. I tried to give myself the permission, dignity, and honor to be alive, worthy of a prepared meal. It was agonizing. It was important. It meant I wasn't going to die with him. I was going to eat my food without him and I would cook again. Being able to eat alone took a long time. I knew it was an acknowledgement of life. I proceeded as if I was going to continue to live on without him.

All the things a baby has to learn I had to re-teach myself: Eat. Go to bed. Say your prayers. Shut your eyes. Dream. Get up. Bathe. Brush your teeth. Nothing was easy or natural. Everything was difficult and made me tired. Move my body. Sit and stare for awhile. Take a walk. Life without my husband began in the simple routines of being human. "As if" became "it is."

It is possible to start again. Life does get easier. I needed to hear those words. I say them now to you.

If the loss you grieve is a death, it doesn't mean you are going to die now, too. Taking care of your own health will make your grief easier. You'll feel better and it's something that's within your control.

Do you avoid exercise? Try to add 20 minutes of walking into your day whenever you can. Walking is not only good for your body, it is a good antidote to depression and anxiety. You can walk away mild depression.

Is it hard for me to take care of myself while I grieve? What has been most difficult for me?

_____

_____

_____

_____

_____

_____

_____

_____

_____

When do I sit down at the table and eat healthy meals?

_____

_____

What healthy choices have I made?

_____

How do I get the exercise I need?

_____

_____

_____

_____

Listen to your dream guide.

My sisters and I sprawled in the living room, still in our flannel night-gowns and ratty slippers. Mom and Dad sat in "their" chairs, coffee in hand. That morning, my sister Carolyn began the ritual:*"Oh, listen to this, last night I dreamed I dropped my camera..."* We listened, asked for details, and talked until each of us had told our dreams. We loved our morning ritual.

When I was 20, I married and moved in with my husband. On our first morning, I got my cup of coffee, sat down in the living room, and began to tell my dream. When I turned to him for his dream, he looked at me with his head tilted, eyes squinted: *"Dream?"* *"Yes,"* I said, *"Don't you tell your dreams?"* He said his idea of a good dream story was *"I dreamt."* Neither of us ever relented our stance.

I enjoy listening to my dreams. My dreamworld has a recurring landscape, present most of my life: a mountain with a river flowing down its side. The river is sometimes whitewater roaring by me as I stand at its edge. At times it moves on a slow meander into a cave at the bottom of the mountain. It changes with moods and events of my life. For example, the day after my husband Greg died, I dreamed that I was standing in the middle of the river, but it was only an inch deep and wider than I could see. There was no mountain in sight; the whole world was flat. It was raining everywhere. This was my first grief dream.

Before my cat Re died, I dreamed I stood in a field with Re in my arms. I held him up to the sky, and his shiny black fur turned to crow feathers. He flew up into the sky and left me. I felt sad but thrilled. Dreams help me grieve.

Although both these dreams used symbols, I knew exactly what they were about without words or explanation. I keep them in a dream journal so I can remember or examine them later, perhaps years later. I also keep a dream journal because it's *fun*.

Dreams are my "nightwork," my subconscious knocking at my conscious to be understood. I believe listening to dreams is a way of listening to God. They are a gift which some prefer to leave untouched and unexamined. Perhaps a private, gentle transcription of a dream is better for you, a ritual of dream writing, or silent dream meditation.

Image substitution: a method to study your dreams

Each of us is our own best dream interpreter. There are other resources that are helpful, but the first and best source for your dream is you.

A therapist showed me a way of understanding my dreams better. The method is easy and enlightening. With it, I can use revealed dream wisdom in my conscious life. This method of studying dreams is sometimes referred to as "image substitution."

There are five steps in the process:

1. Write your dream in all its detail, in the original sequence.

2. Review what you have written and circle each of the (details) that appeared in the dream – objects, people, places.

3. In a column beside the dream story, write words or phrases you associate with the dream details in corresponding order to the original dream. For example:

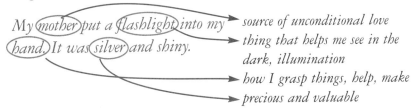

4. Rewrite the dream and substitute all the new associated words for the circled words. Don't worry about clunky sentences; the meaning will come through. Enter it into your journal; then read it out loud. I like to use this method with a trusted friend. We transcribe for each other and then read the dream back to the dreamer with the new words. It may surprise you when you hear your dream in a new voice. From the example above:
    My source of unconditional love put a thing that helps me see in the dark, illumination, into how I grasp things, help, make. It was precious and valuable...

5. Symbols link me to the rest of humanity. I use dream and symbol books to find more clues to the knowledge in my dreams. From the sample above I might look up "silver" or "hand" to see what it has meant in mythology or other cultures. Your dream is yours; weigh the book's ideas against your intuition.

Some additional dreamwork suggestions:

- *Write down your dream as soon as you wake. Write down its details before you get out of bed. Details are helpful, full of meaning, and disappear quickly.*

- *Observe a recurring theme in a series of dreams. The theme may reveal more than an individual dream.*

- *Describe how you felt while in the dream.*

- *Give your dream a title.*

Now, write down a dream you've had while working in this journal. If you don't remember a recent dream, ask for one before you go to sleep tonight. Ask for what help you need from your dream as you lay your head down. Or, try an old folk tradition: eat garlic or put a shell under your pillow for memorable dreams. You will dream.

Date:

Title:

The Dream:	*Associated Words*

The Dream: *Associated Words*

_____|_____
_____|_____
_____|_____
_____|_____
_____|_____
_____|_____
_____|_____
_____|_____
_____|_____
_____|_____
_____|_____
_____|_____

The Dream Retold:

_____
_____
_____
_____
_____
_____
_____
_____
_____
_____
_____

The lost dream

They said,
"You and Greg were so lucky. You had more than some people ever have."

I said,
"What if you had a million dollars last week, but you lost it. Does it help that you once had a million or does that make the loss worse?"

This 'lost million' question went hand in hand with two others:

Question #1: *Why?*
That one began the day after his death. *Why did he die? Why did this happen to us? Why him? Why now?*

Question #2: *Is a memory something I have or something I have lost?*

I asked myself those questions for about 10 years. I found my answers (*See page 81*), but like my high school algebra book with its answers printed in the back, the answers didn't help unless I went through the steps to get there. No one could find my answers for me, nor I for you.

The dream

My questions all shared the same root: the lost dream. Even now, I cry as I write the words: *We didn't get to grow old together.* This is the kernel of my grief.

This was our dream: he would be a curmudgeon and write, and I'd be an eccentric old bat and paint. We'd do it together in our dream house with a porch and fireplace. He'd have a real cook's kitchen, and I'd have a painting studio. We thought if we always challenged ourselves, stayed in touch with young people, and encouraged our creativity, we'd have a great old age. We never even got as far as a house.

We were born a month apart: Greg is still 33; I'm now 49. The gap continues to widen. The gap isn't a void, and I'm grateful for the intervening years. Now, I am the keeper of the lost dream.

To think about or write out your lost dream may be more difficult than other parts of this grief journal. If this is the kernel of your grief, remember that, like all seeds, the lost dream may hold new life inside.

I've asked this question again and again since it happened:

_____

_____

_____

This is the dream I lost:

_____

_____

_____

_____

_____

_____

_____

_____

_____

_____

_____

_____

_____

_____

_____

_____

_____

_____

These are the other dreams I have lost throughout my life:

O, *night of starry water...*

Our church was steeped in ritual. Even as a young child I knew the drill: *stand up for the processional, sit down for the lesson, kneel for the prayer, say the creed out loud...* I knew how to do it by rote but not by heart, because, for me, there was no heart connection. When I became a teenager, I refused to follow along. I no longer said things I didn't understand or believe – I still won't. I stopped going to church because I thought I hated ritual.

But I loved ritual that was personal. It was present in my life from the beginning. From the time my big sisters first bounced me on their knees and taught me their songs, I wanted to be what they were – *Campfire Girls!* They sang old songs about the beauty of God's earth and the mystery and wonder of life. I, too, became a Campfire Girl and marked passages in my young life with beautiful ceremonies. We honored work, health and love with beads, rings, and songs. I looked for my own talents, renamed myself *(O wa ma me ga),* and began the dream of who I am.

Campfire Girl rituals weren't empty repetitions of words drilled into me, but deep, deliberate, and thoughtful poems, music, and movement which I helped choose and form. I found the presence of peace, truth, beauty, and love: God. This experience formed a deep well in the ground of my soul. And it was still there waiting for me a quarter of a century later when I needed it.

I needed it to help me with my husband's ashes. Each night for the first two months after he died, I sat on the sofa in his blue, terry-cloth robe and cried puddles onto the box that held his ashes. (I hadn't known tears could make puddles.) It was time for me to release the ashes. Greg wasn't one for symbol or ritual, but I needed to do something

O, night of starry water,

today you're in the sand.

I'll keep your spirit with me,

I'll try to understand.

that was right and good for both of us, something sacred. So, with my sister Judy as acolyte, I drew from that old childhood well and made a ritual. She was firemaker and torchbearer. I stood high on a rocky ledge, close to the water's edge, and cast his bones into the Lake Superior cove that he loved. His bone ash in my hands was startling with its many colors and surprising weight. As I touched the insides of his bones, I felt the most intimate moment of our relationship. Flung into the cove in moonlight and fire sparks, I watched him fill the bottom of the cove with underwater stars. We swirled his molecules back into the earth with songs of love. We danced with God that night.

Your ritual.

Now, in middle age, those same rote rituals that chafed me as a teen comfort me and bring me joy. I need both the ritual of my church and the ritual that I make for myself. Ritual makes an act as simple as brushing my teeth or as complex as spreading ashes a live connection between God and my life. Ritual-making may already be an important part of your life. If making your own ritual is new for you, here are some suggestions you might find helpful.

Like the choreography of a prayer, ritual has form, place, and time. It's three dimensional. It has a beginning, middle, and end, during which it moves and takes form. You might consider these basic elements:

What: Name your ritual. What is it?
When: Choose a time. How long will it be?
Where: Where are you going to do this? Do you need a sacred spot? Do you need peace? Find the place. Consider privacy or the possible interference of outside noise or distraction.

Gather and prepare. Set the scene – you are your own altar guild. Use whatever objects have sacred or symbolic significance to you. These might include:

candles	water	music	cloth	bread
flowers	vessel	fruit	wine	rock
bible	shawl	bell	cross	sage
drum	fire	incense	oil	poetry

Begin — Prepare your soul and state of mind.
Be present and set aside other concerns.
Consider an opening blessing or music.
Ask for God's presence.
Light a candle, dip your hands into water, or raise your face to the sun.
This may be done as a blessing to begin your ritual or it may be the ritual.
It is your presence in the action and your deliberateness that matter.

Do it/be it:

pray	chant	sing	dance	paint
walk	meditate	breathe	look	stretch
move	play	make music	cry	bathe
eat	drink	sprinkle water	draw	sing

Make an ending. Give thanks and praise.

These rituals are already a part of my life:

_____

_____

_____

_____

_____

I'd like to have a ritual to help me:

_____

_____

_____

_____

_____

_____

_____

_____

_____

_____

_____

My ritual:

Title: _____

The place:

_____

When and how long:

_____

A thing or object that seems important to include:

_____

_____

_____

_____

_____

The opening or blessing:

_____

_____

_____

The doing:

_____

_____

_____

_____

The closing:

_____

_____

_____

_____

Make the pack lighter.

What are those doing in here? Across the room from me stood a wall of Greg's noisy and eccentric record albums. *He's not coming back to listen to them.* I hadn't noticed them in the room before, even though I was the one who put them there. Some of that music was the soundtrack of our life together – "our" songs. I won't listen to them. The others I never liked and was grateful I didn't have to listen to them again. *Why were they still in my living room?*

I was blind until I was ready to see. Then I saw my home was full of monuments dedicated to Greg. Two thousand comic books, his guitar on the wall, his favorite box of electronic junk, his defunct computer, special cookware – I had all these relics in my home and he never even lived there. I had carried his junk with me through two moves. *Oh man!* As my eyes began to see, my heart admitted he wouldn't be back for his stuff. I didn't like the truth: death is non-negotiable.

I lived in the mausoleum of my dead husband for years. A mausoleum isn't a good place for life. I had decided to live, so I began to make decisions about what I could release. With a lot of letting go, I condensed a houseful of his remains to one dresser top "altar" of his relics.

Late one night somewhere in Tennessee on a cross-country trip, I sat in a crowded depot next to a stranger, another widow. As she tried to gauge where I was in my grief process, she asked where I kept *his* picture. When I told her it was on the dresser, she suggested I move it, step by step... to the back of the dresser, up on a shelf, to the back of the shelf, into the closet, into a box. She was blunt and honest with me. *I condensed the mess to one altar; wasn't that enough?* I knew what she said rang true. When I returned, I dismantled the altar and started to move it step by step as she suggested.

Now I have one homemade heart-shaped box that contains his remains: a few of his ashes, a couple photos, a letter – the last intimate fragments of our life together. It's in a closet on a high shelf. I don't open it often and it's manageable – smaller than a breadbox. I gave his things away to family, friends, and charities. Some things I burned; others went in the trash. My home became mine and for the first time everything in it belonged to me. I made it a lighter, easier place to live.

How does my home reflect who I am now?

_____

_____

_____

What junk have I been holding on to?

_____

_____

_____

_____

How do I feel about moving things, step by step, into the background?

_____

_____

_____

_____

LINDA LODGE ASCLOPN

Look in the shadows.

The patient said outrageous things as they wheeled her down the hall to the operating room; she was under the influence of pre-op sedation, had no inhibitions, and was swearing a blue streak. She embarrassed her husband and the attendants, but they couldn't stop her. I knew the woman whose demons came out on the gurney, and if it could happen to her, it could happen to me.

With her story ringing in my ears I dreaded my first surgery. I feared my dark thoughts and what bad words might leap out of my mouth. *What's inside me that's waiting to get out? What secrets, shame, and guilt lurk in my corners?* I could think of some things, but even my journal wasn't safe enough to hold them, so the night before I went under anesthesia I put all my fears and scary thoughts into a tiny rubbery monster doll. I let the doll hold them all. I also asked God to cast out my scary thoughts in the name of Jesus. It worked – I didn't say anything unusual and the surgery went fine, but I remember that fear of what might be inside me.

I'm not going to tell you my most private, dark thoughts, but I can share an example. I felt relief when my mother died – not the general gratefulness that her pain was over, but my personal relief and freedom because I no longer had to explain myself to her, justify my actions, or live up to her dream of who I should be. Then, because I loved my mother, I felt guilty for those feelings, as if I had wished her dead. Death-wish guilt may lurk in the background after a loved one dies, especially if the relationship was intense, difficult, or complex.

The "shadow" is a (Jungian) name for a part of me (and all of us) that lies beneath the surface. I often deny or reject that part, but it makes me whole or balanced. When I acknowledge my shadow, it won't lurk in the background to steal my energy or suddenly appear to demand attention when I'm most vulnerable. It loses its power to scare me.

Consider looking at your shadow. Be careful. Use your prayer of safety and protection before you begin to write. Try writing with your non-dominant hand to help release your inner voice. If you have complete privacy, you can write on the following pages. When you finish, fold it over and even staple it. Otherwise, use a separate piece of paper. Burn or shred it if you need to release it.

What part of myself is the most difficult part for me to like or accept?

_____

_____

_____

_____

_____

_____

_____

_____

_____

_____

_____

_____

_____

_____

_____

_____

Who brings out my intense negative feelings?

_____

_____

_____

_____

_____

_____

How might this relate to a part of myself I don't like or accept?

_____

_____

_____

_____

_____

_____

_____

_____

_____

_____

_____

_____

_____

_____

_____

_____

_____

What's inside me that's waiting to get out? What secrets, shame, or guilt lurk in my corners?

_____

_____

_____

_____

_____

_____

_____

_____

_____

_____

What that I consider negative or dangerous in my feelings might offer greater wholeness or balance in my life?

_____

_____

_____

_____

_____

_____

_____

_____

_____

_____

_____

_____

Nap on a warm rock.

The sea is dark and turbulent under a low gray-green sky. A wave hits the prow of my rowboat and I hunker down, shoulders into the wind, eyes shut against the force and vibration. My boat dips into the next trough in expectation of the wave to come, but it doesn't. My eyes open a crack and I see my desk is in front of me, dry and still; I have survived the pain. I can put aside the image of the boat in the stormy sea and go on with my work. I won't need it again for a while.

The image came from a Winslow Homer painting. When I first saw *The Fog Warning*, I knew in a flash that this painting looked like my pain. I could use the image and enter into it for help. I was learning to take help where I found it, especially after I stopped using alcohol. When I go *through* pain, rather than avoid it or push it under, I live it out and it stops. It's the most direct route to calm.

The image in the painting guided me through pain. I have another image that helps me with anxiety. I found it on a crisp early spring afternoon, while deep in a forest wilderness. I was clearing a trail and had never been so deep in the woods alone; it was exhilarating. The path opened onto a rocky ledge with miles of pristine lake and forest spread out before me. The sun sparkled on the water far below, the tips of the pines waved in the wind, the sky beamed blue under a golden sun; it was glorious. I laid down on the ledge and fell asleep with the sun on my face. The rock radiated healing warmth through my back and clean cool air breathed peace in me. It was the best nap I've ever taken.

I often recapture that nap; I can grab it in a heartbeat. I shut my eyes and feel the warm rock beneath me. I remember the water-sparkle, the trees, and the sky. I let the sun of God's healing warmth surround me and fill me with love. That image relieves my anxiety and brings me peace.

What would my pain look like if I saw it in a painting?

_____

_____

_____

_____

_____

_____

_____

_____

What is the most beautiful and relaxing moment in my life? These are the
details of what I felt and saw:

_____

_____

_____

_____

_____

_____

_____

_____

_____

_____

_____

Composting leftovers

My fingers walked over the shoulders of each shirt in my closet. There was one that made my jaw tense, my heart sink – a blue, tropical-flowered shirt. I paused and sighed over that blue shirt each day. It was my torment. The happiest moments in his life were spent in that shirt – mine, too. The major clean-out of his relics was done. This shirt was so much a part of our happiness that I hadn't considered getting rid of it. *Did that shirt have to live in my closet for the rest of my life? No!* I had an idea and I also had a good therapist who inspired my plan and listened to my process. The first stage was talking it through. I devised a ritual. I hoped to transform the pain of the good memory locked inside the shirt – like composting.

My garden tomatoes needed stakes and ties, so I ripped the shirt into long thin pieces, got down on my knees in the dirt, and started remembering. As I tied the plants, I finally let myself think about Greg and the trip where we got that shirt. The best memories are the hardest to think about. But tying, feeling each green plant, smelling the dirt was good ground for remembrance. Soon, each tomato plant wore a blue and white flowered bow tie.

Next, I pulled up a chair beside the garden, turned on the hose, and watered the tomatoes. My therapist, Stephen, told me I wouldn't cry forever. I only believed him because I trusted him. Water was good accompaniment for tears; it felt good. I sang the song I made after I scattered Greg's ashes. *O, night of starry water... remember how happy he looked as he fed those gulls, listened to Carmina Burana, and smiled at me in the wind...* Water hit my cheeks and soaked the plants' new ties.

The tomatoes looked cheery. This and that in the garden needed adjustment. I forgot to sing and cry and became involved with the garden; I moved a rock, straightened a stick, and came into awareness of the present. Stephen was right: I *hadn't* cried forever, probably not even 10 minutes. Greg's shirt became support for new life. I thought about a good memory and re-entered the world in the present moment.

Over the years I used those ties for other tomatoes until they faded to grey and began to decompose. Their molecules mixed with the soil, entered the plants, and grew into flowers. Or maybe I ate them in a sandwich.

If weighty symbols of the past, either good or bad, torment you, you can choose to transform them. Sometimes a coat of paint will do the trick. Turn a pot upside down and it becomes a pedestal. An old gold ring can be melted into a new form. Stones can be reset.

Consider composting your leftovers: look in your closet, drawer, or cupboard.

Am I living with a painful symbol, something laden with old memories? Can I let it go? Can I transform it into something else?

_____

_____

_____

_____

Here's how I can use it in a different way:

_____

_____

_____

_____

_____

_____

_____

_____

_____

_____

_____

_____

_____

Happens / Gone

Our leader made a single clap and said, "Happens." He opened his hands, held them wide, and said, "Gone." Throughout the week of that business seminar, he repeated: *happens/gone, happens/gone.* With that phrase and gesture he urged us to take responsibility for the present moment.

How do I hold onto the present moment that is gone as soon as it happens? Why do I want to? As I age, I notice time moves faster. If I pay attention, in the present moment, life becomes denser, with the details in focus. But, "now" is like a bird on the wing or smiles; I can't hold on to them. I can "be with." When I notice the moment and savor it, life is rich and long.

To live in the present moment is also a way to handle fear, anxiety, and grief. For example, last year I got through fear of surgery with the phrase "I'm not there yet, I don't have to think about that now." That took me right up to the operating room. Then, I used an image, every detail from my rocky ledge nap (*See "Nap on a warm rock"*) to hold me in God's healing warmth. It worked. I both separated myself from fear with an image, and I stayed in the present moment.

In times of high anxiety, such as war and international crisis, I live in the present moment and it helps. To imagine all the possible outcomes, whether in an operating room or a war, can lead me down a scary path where life is out of my control. I don't need to walk down that path.

This moment right now is where I am. *Happens, gone.* I can fly beside the bird and smile with the child. Whether I'm on a shuttle bus and notice the people with me, or on a beach with salt on my lips, if I'm fully present, I own that moment for life.

This moment, I smell coffee, hear the children next door, feel pain in my knee, see dots of yellow leaves falling sideways in the air. Box elder bugs crawl on the screen. *Happens, gone.* Perhaps the greatest lesson from the loss is *happens, gone.* So, now is the time to wear your best shoes and eat off the good dishes. Don't wait. Enjoy the present. Do you know what time the sun rose today? Enter into the moment.

To begin, set this book down. Without talking or moving, shut your eyes and listen for five minutes. Become aware of every sound and movement around you. Then, open your eyes, look for five minutes. Notice everything.

I captured 10 minutes. This is what I saw and heard...

_____

_____

_____

_____

_____

_____

_____

_____

_____

_____

_____

_____

_____

Betrayal

Who will love Greg if I move on with my life? If I live in marriage with another man, what will happen to Greg? Does this mean I didn't love him enough? How can I hold two men in my heart at the same time? I keep a part of Greg's spirit around me. How can I do that as another man's wife?

As I prepared to marry John, I felt confusion and guilt – a betrayer of my first marriage vows. Although my first vows clearly said we would part at death, I had hoped to be with him again someday, which brought up another problem. When all three of us are dead, whose wife will I be? Who will I hang around with in eternity?

I lay on the sofa with these thoughts spinning in my head. In two weeks I would marry John. He asked, "What's wrong, honey?"

"What's going to happen to Greg when we get married?" He looked at me and said, "He can live here with us." Those simple words were the kindest words ever spoken to me.

Guilt is a by-product of betrayal. There is reasonable guilt that is a part of taking responsibility for the things we do, but the most common form of guilt is unreasonable and stems from shame. I absolve true guilt when I make amends and ask forgiveness. When I realize and acknowledge unreasonable guilt, I can release it. My feelings that I was betraying Greg were real but based on an unreasonable guilt. I needed to resolve and acknowledge these feelings and not torment myself with guilt.

As my guilt was resolved, I became free to love again.

When I think about moving on with my life, I feel...

I have feelings of unreasonable guilt regarding...

What reasonable guilt do I own for which I need to ask forgiveness or make amends?

_____

_____

_____

_____

_____

_____

_____

_____

_____

_____

_____

_____

_____

_____

_____

_____

I forgive myself for...

_____

_____

_____

_____

_____

_____

_____

_____

All in one being

I look back: *she sat at the dining room table, up in the sky, looking out at the clouds. The 9th floor apartment had windows floor to ceiling across the front of the living room and dining room. From where she sat all she could see was sky. She held the cool edge of a wineglass against her lips and stared.* Is he out there somewhere? *She felt blank. Not a gentle release as in meditation, but blank like she just lost half her soul. She was still in shock; her husband, Greg, had died in the next room just a couple of days before. A constant vibration ran through her body, and her ears rang in anticipation of pain to come. But, rather than pain, she began to feel held — lifted and comforted. The comfort puzzled and amazed her.*

The comfort I received doesn't puzzle me now. When I look back at myself and see that dining room scene, I stand outside of myself, look on, and pray for "her." Other people said they were praying for me that day. I believe it.

Coil Theory

I see time, or my being in time, as a golden coil. I imagine something like a bedspring, a golden one, turning slowly. Each loop in the spring marks a year. Marked along its edge is the timeline of my life – all of my hours, days, months, and years. A point marks the present moment from which my lifetime spirals down to my first heartbeat and loops up into the unknown future. The coil is my whole life at once. This image is my mind's-eye view of my existence in time – *Lodge's Coil Theory.*

My coil of time is pliable. It bends, compresses, and recoils in an unpredictable manner. How often a minute has seemed to last an hour – a year, a day. Moments in my life have felt connected with something in my future. Other times I live out what I remember I knew a long time ago. I feel the relativity of time – and it's not a straight line.

Several years after the deaths of my husband and mother, I began a kind of prayer that sprang from my coil image of time. I remembered the day I looked at the clouds and experienced strength and comfort in my time of loss and desperation.

I believe this strength and comfort came from God, and that by praying, we join our energy and spirit with God's. I always feel strength when other people pray for me. It changed my life that first time I felt their prayers lift me.

So, now I add my prayers to the prayers that were prayed for me. I bend my coil down, like pinching the side of the spring, until I feel connected with me in that past moment. Then retroactively, I pray. I send a prayer back to me then, from me now.

Each of our brains sorts life and information differently. How do you see time inside your imagination? Do you ever feel a connection with another time? Have you ever prayed for something in the past?

This is how I see or feel the years of my life inside my head.

_____

_____

_____

_____

There is a time I received comfort from other people praying for me.
It was when...

_____

_____

_____

I'd like to add this prayer to the help I received when I was in pain.

_____

_____

_____

_____

_____

_____

Anger

I didn't know I was angry.

It was a late summer evening when I first walked down the Soo Line trail, an old railroad bed through the woods and lush wetlands. I was alone on the road, and scared. The trail stretched ahead, but when I looked behind, trees obscured my entry point. Through the narrowing "V" of trees ahead, I saw a spot of golden light. The bushes beside me trembled and in the shadows in front of me something moved. *What if that's a blood-thirsty lunatic with a knife?* I pivoted and bolted back to the safety of my hermitage at The Dwelling in the Woods. I would go back in the morning to see what was out there. *What was that opening of golden light?*

The next morning I was prepared. My shoes had hard bottoms and I felt courage and excitement. The sun was still behind the trees somewhere, and a layer of fog padded the morning light. I felt at ease with the woods beside me as I walked the old railroad bed trail. The light darkened in the deep green tunnel. Only the crunch of my boots on the gravel broke the still and quiet of the morning. Something shimmered in the distance.
This time I strode into the light: *Oooh!*

You made the pain,

You made the sorrow,

so, help me now,

hold me close,

I'm here alone on this road!

I was stunned by the panorama of beauty spread out before me. It was as if I stood before the face of God. Rays of gold light beamed down through pink mist. Emotion rose inside me as I stood face to face with God. I found myself angry. I was <u>mad</u>, mad as hell! I raised my fist and shook it. You!
You made the pain. You made the sorrow. So, HELP me now, hold me close, I'm here alone on this road!

It was a song and it burst out of me complete with words and music.

This was new. I didn't even know I was mad. I certainly didn't know I had a song inside me to accompany my anger. My parents didn't allow anger in our family. Nice girls didn't get mad. We had no choice about that.

After my husband's death, people told me again and again I was angry, but I denied it. In fact I was depressed. I knew that depression was related to repressed anger, but I couldn't get hold of it. I finally stopped arguing with my friends and agreed, "O.K. I'm angry." These were empty words so people would leave me alone. Until the moment when I was face to face with God in that glorious panorama on the trail, I didn't believe I was angry. I never expected beauty would be the key to releasing my anger.

Anger is reasonable, and a recognized stage of grief. Elizabeth Kubler-Ross, in her book, *On Death and Dying,* puts grief into five stages: denial and isolation, anger, bargaining, depression, and acceptance. I've found that people sometimes use this information to label other people in grief in a way that is dismissive of their current feelings. Recognition of these stages is helpful – it helped me believe I wasn't alone in this process. And it gave me hope that acceptance would come.

How easy or difficult is it for me to acknowledge my anger?

_____

_____

_____

I've felt so much anger about...

_____

_____

_____

_____

_____

_____

_____

_____

_____

When I'm angry, I...

I believe a healthy and non-violent way to express my anger is to...

Anger in my family was...

_____

_____

_____

_____

_____

_____

_____

_____

_____

_____

I remember a time someone else's anger hurt me. It was when...

_____

_____

_____

_____

_____

_____

_____

_____

Do I have a problem with anger? Do I need to discuss it with a therapist?

_____

_____

_____

_____

_____

Life in the forest

So, there I was, a couple miles into the woods on the Soo Line trail, shouting my song and shaking my fist at God. I turned back on the trail and as I walked I sang the song over and over again to the rhythm of my stomping feet: *You made the pain, You made the sorrow, so help me now, hold me close, I'm here alone on this road.* I picked, or rather yanked, wildflowers along the way and held them in my arms. When I returned to my hermitage retreat cabin, I gathered a blanket, flute, cookies, and journal and took them with my wildflowers into the nearby woods. I laid the blanket on the ground and sat down to stew my anger and weave.

My mother was a weaver, and I remembered an old picture of her, little Jean, weaving flowers into a head wreath. I cried remembering her smile of innocent delight; she was my guide that day. I wove my own head wreath and, as I wove, I continued to sing my "Angry at God" song. I transcribed the song and played it on my flute. I hadn't played for years but it sounded good in the woods.

Squirrels sniffed around me, birds sang above, and a buck crashed through the bushes. Throughout the day other hermits wandered by as their paths merged or crossed mine. They moved silently to the tune of their own inner journey's song. We were alone together. Life is abundant with fellow travellers in the forest.

At sunset I walked again to the Trail of the Angry Song. I had my flute and no fear of lunatics. I played my Angry Song as I watched the sun set. The sun set on my anger as it set on the day.

Before dawn, I packed my paints and headed out to paint the face of God as I had seen it the day before. *Oh, what a painting that would be!* An hour up the trail in fog, through the deep green V, I found the spot. But, there was no gold. This time the spot looked the same as the place on the trail where I started an hour back. I chuckled and sat down to paint pastel hues of fog and my song returned with changed words. My fist unclenched, palms opened, a new verse appeared:

> *You made the sun,*
> *You gave me hope,*
> *You cried with me,*
> *Held me close,*
> *I'm here with You on this road.*

Later I joined the other hermits around a table for lunch. We each had our stories to tell. In such table-talk, perhaps one of us says just the words another needs. Perhaps a stranger becomes a friend. Seven years earlier, I couldn't have imagined the path to this table of friendly strangers. I didn't know how to get there or that a table of such nourishment even existed. Now, like the solution to a maze, it's easy to look back from the inside and see how each step led to the next and made my path. I am grateful for the first steps I blindly took. They got me here.

Since your loss, you may find your old communities no longer fit you the same way. Or, perhaps you've discovered new depth in a familiar community. Consider following a call you've never answered. Spiritual communities, environmental groups, retreat centers, dance groups, choirs, poetry workshops, bird clubs – what is calling you? Seek it out, let your heart sing with others – you may discover your new voice.

Does my soul have a community in which to thrive?

_____

_____

_____

_____

_____

Does my heart hear a call I've never answered? What is it?

_____

_____

_____

_____

_____

_____

_____

_____

_____

_____

_____

As I've walked down my path of grief toward healing, I have discovered this along the way...

_____

_____

_____

_____

_____

_____

_____

_____

_____

_____

_____

_____

_____

_____

I've learned this about myself...

Rewrite history.

On the first night of the silent Lenten retreat the priest gave us a task: *"Find the hurt and go to it."* Back in my room I lit a candle, prayed, and shut my eyes. I went way back into the dark. *Oh, there it is.* I began to write in my journal, and the night unfolded. I saw a child in a slope-roofed, back bedroom, far away from the rest of the family. It was three o'clock in the morning, a desolate time with so many hours to get through until dawn. Her eyes were wide open, straining to see in the dark, afraid to blink. Sweat prickled her forehead, her stomach churned, but she wouldn't call out for help.

Bear, penguin, tiger, and lamb were in bed with her; they didn't have names, but she loved them. She pulled them around her and made a bedspread tent. She turned the flashlight on and began the club meeting with her unnamed friends. Sometimes it lasted until dawn – sleep came easily with the first pink light. *Why didn't she call out when she was scared?* Oh, sometimes she did, and her mom or dad showed her the closet was empty and nothing was under the bed. Most times, she suffered alone – with her animals.

As I wrote in my journal, the memory of fear came back to me. Now I knew how to get through fear without waiting for the dawn. I knew how to pray, and I had discovered my "golden coil," so I could go back in time to help me. I could pray for the child I once was and then rewrite history.

With the help of my journal, I went back to that dark night and relived it a different way. This time, I called out for help, *"Mommy, I'm scared."* Mother came into the room and sat down beside me, smoothed my forehead, and said, *"I used to be scared of the dark, too. Let's pray together. Jesus will help us get through the night. He's right here with us now."* Mom never prayed spontaneously with me, didn't know I needed those words, or how to say them. She would have if she had known how. Now, I can go back anytime and she's there with me, smoothing my forehead and praying with me. It's a truth even if it didn't happen that way.

Rewriting history isn't about denial; I can't go back and change the fact that Greg's heart valve prolapsed. But I can go back and be with him in spirit as he sat down on the floor and died. I can redo what happened within myself and bring comfort, strength and love where needed.

You, too, can write a new version of an old painful story. It's possible for it to be true even if it didn't happen. Consider rewriting your history.

Find the hurt, deep inside, and go to it.

_____

_____

_____

_____

_____

_____

_____

_____

_____

_____

_____

_____

_____

_____

_____

_____

_____

_____

_____

_____

_____

_____

_____

Say farewell.

I was married to a dead man, and it wasn't going too well. After nine years I still hadn't said goodbye. I wanted my freedom. At the end of an intense *Beginning Experience** weekend retreat, I wrote a letter of farewell to my husband, Greg. The letter was a catharsis and cleared space around my heart. I put this letter in the box of his relics high up on the shelf in my closet.

As I near the end of this *Grief Journal,* the box is down and open again. My sister Christine made the heart-shaped cardboard container that holds Greg's relics, the detritus of a life – a few bone shards, a ring, a clay rabbit, a photo of a little blonde boy with long arms. The letter rises like white wings.

August 1995.

My dear Bozo Bean, oh Grego, why did you leave! No... I know you didn't want to go either. Did your body choose a time when I wasn't there because I couldn't have stopped you? I was so upset that you died without me. Then I came to believe, and I believe now that you were not alone.

You know my heart; you know my loss; you know what we had. After nine years without you, I know why I never took that love for granted. We always knew we were lucky. Even when we had trouble, we still had a lot. We loved so hard, so easy.

Will you forgive me for making you cry about _____ ? You know I'm sorry. We didn't get a chance to laugh about it before you died. Grego, I'm getting old without you, and I can't hear your voice anymore. I still know your eyes, though. Will you help me? I'm trying to move on.

We were a guitar. You were the strings; I was the body. The strings broke; your strings always broke. I remember you on stage with strings flying off the the bridge as you played. God played our life on that guitar. God needed us to play the song. The strings usually break first, especially with your music. I've let the strings hang there. I want to unwind them. I'm ready. What do I do with a stringless guitar? What's left... a drum? Maybe someone else will know how to string this old guitar someday.

My love, I will remember the song and the music. It was beautifully played. I'm taking the strings out now; I'm ready. Forgive me; bless me. Our love is an ancient love. There's so much good in my life that came from your death, thank you. Your ashes are the soil of my new growth. You are part of my soul.

Goodbye my love, Linda.

---

* Beginning Experience is a program designed to help widowed, separated, and divorced persons make a new beginning in life.

This morning I wrote another letter to him, I had new things to say. Over the years, old boyfriends, my parents, former bosses, and my cat Re all got letters. I mailed some, but most stayed in my journal.

Consider writing a letter of farewell, even if you don't think there's anything else to say to the person. You may be surprised. The letter I shared with you has been scrubbed of intimate detail, and I have put it into readable sentences. If you know you can't or won't mail it, don't worry about how you write – say what needs to be said.

You could send your letter by ritual post: burn it and send a smoke signal, make a letter-boat and float it into a river, or, put it underground in a garden and let it grow. Consider mailing it to yourself. Send it in a way that is symbolic or meaningful for you.

If you write your letter intending to send it to the person you wrote it to, I suggest that you wait a couple days before you put it in the mail. Give yourself a chance to reconsider: is it necessary to mail it? Are you trying to re-engage in a relationship that's over? Remember, the healing catharsis of the letter happens within yourself as you write. Its purpose isn't to injure or fix the other person.

If you are ready, there is a place on the next page to write your letter. You may want to use a separate sheet of paper if you plan to mail it with ritual or the post office.

Am I ready to say farewell?

_____

Will I send the letter? How?

_____

_____

_____

_____

Farewell

Epilogue

To you, the other writer in this journal

The pines look black at dusk as they crowd together beyond the trail. Once, in another dusk, I had hurried by them in a cold sweat, thinking I was lost. Now I claim them: I belong to the Pine Cathedral.

I used to paint these tall pines from across the meadow. When at last I had the courage to leave the trail, I discovered my most sacred spot: my home, my center. The only line from catechism that has stuck with me from childhood is the definition of a sacrament – "an outward and visible sign of an inward and spiritual grace." Yes. These trees are me, inside: big and dark with spokes of branches that will poke your eye out, but the bottom is soft; its thick cushion, a century of needles, upholstered in green moss. Above, the blue dome wears a black lace veil of mourning.

Last night I returned to the cathedral. Dressed in fluorescent orange vestments, I processed into the bramble vestibule jangling a tambourine of hiking bells to the songs I taught myself on my grief journey – the "Angry Song" and "O, night of starry water." On a previous visit I had discovered a large quartz crystal in a rock pile. It was still there on the low altar stone where I left it.

I claim it now. I bring it out into the world, into the light. It's a gift. It is a gift of freedom. I had thought a gift of freedom meant being in a loving relationship again and discovered that the loving relationship needed to be with myself. This rock is an outward and visible sign of finding my center, my heart, and sharing it in partnership with you.

Your words are invisible to me, but I hope you, too, have filled this book, so it has also become a book about you. I hope you burst out of this journal and begin another, all your own, as you have opened doors that need more room for your thoughts and feelings.

Resurrection

The path of my journey moved from the deaths in my life to a new place in the center of the forest. It was there all along. Grief became a journey to myself. Before 9:32 p.m., May 12, 1986, I didn't consciously know any of the things about myself that I have written in this journal. I had a good marriage and a happy life. We had fun. I also drank a lot, worked too much, watched TV every day, and had no spiritual life. I had an inkling there was more. I found it because Greg died.

The loss of everything I knew and held dear gave me two things that can never be taken from me: my sobriety and my companionship with God. I will never be alone in that same black hole where I whispered my first real prayer: "Help!"

Greg's death gave me life.

Life is good. *Amen.*

The resurrection in my loss is...

_____

_____

_____

_____

_____

_____

_____

Answers in the back of the book

My answers. (from page 38)

Yes, I'm glad I had a million dollars. It's not gone, it's been converted into richness within me.

#1. Why? Why not?

A friend, an avowed atheist, asked me "Linda, how can you believe in God after what happened to Greg?" Aside from being struck by what sounded more like anger at God than disbelief in God, I felt an epiphany of understanding: Greg's death wasn't bad. It took me four years to get to that. Thirty-three years was the length of his life. It is neither good nor bad; it just is. "Justice, just is." I don't need to ask why anymore.

#2. A memory is both something I've lost and something I keep. I've learned to be all in one being. I am 3, I am 80, I am 49. I am all of me at once. What I once had in physical reality I now hold present in my soul. Everything still lives within me. I have my whole life.

Acknowledgements

I'm grateful to:

- my publisher, Joan Mitchell, at Good Ground Press, for saying "yes" to *Grief Journal*. This book wanted to be written. Joan's trust, encouragement and guidance allowed it to come into the world.
- my editor, close friend, and favorite poet, Carol Pearce Bjorlie. Carol improved my writing and helped find the words to match what was in my heart.
- my friend Patty Murtaugh for the ham sandwich and a thousand other acts of kindness.
- my friend Andrew Mackenzie, of Mackenzie Marketing Inc., for his advice and encouragement.
- my friend David Vergeyle, of Imagicast Inc., for the computer and for the opportunity of change.
- Chris Loegering and Julie DeLange for their spiritual guidance before and after death.
- Dr. Stephen Huey for his wise, kind, and creative therapy.
- all my friends at the Dwelling in the Woods: Jean Stodola, Kirsten Vogt, Connie Delgado, Carol Simonson, Marion Klaus, Joan Baron, Whisper, and Smudge.
- all my fellow wounded healers in *Beginning Experience*, *Befrienders*, and *A.A.*
- the friends who were with me at the time of Greg's death: Jean Lodge, Ingrid Miza, Susan Abelson, Peter Johnson, Frank and Robin Schreiber, Mary Ann Fimrite, Patty Murtaugh, Carol Lysak, Lois Bjorlie, Onno Kremers.
- my daily email circle of Camp Fire Girl friends, Barb Williams, Sandy Johnson, Judy Lodge, and Carolyn Guthrie, for their encouragement, ideas, and cheers.
- my first in-laws, Harold and LaDonna Abelson, for their support and love.
- my in-laws, Phillip and Adaline Andreozzi, for their support and love.
- my husband John and my sisters Judy, Carolyn, and Christine for their belief in me and for being a part of my life forever.

Resources

The books, tapes, and music I have listed below helped me through the forest of my grief. There were many others, but these, like my one-eyed Teddy Bear from childhood, were cherished and held often. The book covers are scuffed and worn, their insides underlined and tear-stained. The tapes are stretched, the voices waver. The CDs are caseless from constant play. They have been lent, traded, given away, and replaced again and again. I think they're all great.

Books

A Grief Observed – C.S. Lewis

Alcoholics Anonymous – Alcoholics Anonymous World Services Inc.

Manual for Beginning Experience – Sr. Josephine Stewart, Sr. Karen Lay, Fr. E. Guy Gau

Care of the Soul – Thomas Moore

Each Day a New Beginning, Daily Meditations for Women – Hazelden

The Essene Book of Days – Danaan Parry

Feeling Good – Dr. David Burns, M.D.

First Prayers – Tasha Tudor

Flying Without Fear – Duane Brown, Ph.D.

Forgiveness – Syrup Bergan & S. Marie Schwan

Good Grief Rituals, Tools for Healing – Elaine Childs-Gowell A.R.N.P., Ph.D.

Interbeing, Fourteen Guidelines for Engaged Buddhism – Thich Nhat Hanh

The Jerusalem Bible, Reader's Edition – Alexander Jones, Editor

Jesus: The Son of Man – Kahlil Gibran

Selected Poems of Rainer Maria Rilke – Translation by Robert Bly

Twenty-Four Hours a Day – Harper/Hazelden

The Wind in the Willows – Kenneth Grahame

You Don't Have to Quit – Ann & Ray Ortlund

Tapes

New Seeds of Contemplation – Thomas Merton

Soulmates – Thomas Moore

Music

Adagio – Albinoni

Nocturnes – Chopin

Music for the Soul – Thomas Moore

Dreamstreams – Dean Evenson

Ordering Information

Do you know others who could benefit from *Grief Journal*? Order additional copies by phone, Web site, or mail. Quantity discounts are available.

Also, available – A Group Facilitator Guide.

Grief Journal is a powerful tool for healing in a group setting. This detailed, 6-page, easy-to-follow *Facilitator Guide* can help your parish, retreat center, or other organization use *Grief Journal* in a group setting.

To order more copies of Grief Journal, call toll free:

800-232-5533

Or, visit our Web sites:

griefjournal.com *or* goodgroundpress.com

Or, fill out the coupon below and mail it to:

GRIEF JOURNAL
GOOD GROUND PRESS
1884 RANDOLPH AVENUE,
ST. PAUL, MN 55105

Name:

Title:

Organization:

Street

City: State/Zip:

Phone (work)   Phone (home)

Item	Quantity	Price	Amount Due
Grief Journal (1-10)		$15.95 each	
Grief Journal (11-99)		$13.50 each	
Grief Journal (100 or more)		$10.95 each	
Facilitator Guide		$1.50 each	
		Subtotal	
	Shipping (8% of subtotal, minimum $3.95)		
		Order Total